THANKSGIVING
Holiday Grab Bag

by Judith Stamper

illustrated by Ann Iosa

Troll Associates

METRIC EQUIVALENTS

1 inch = 2.54 centimeters
1 square inch = 6.45 square centimeters
1 foot = 30.5 centimeters

1 teaspoon = 5 milliliters (approx.)
1 tablespoon = 15 milliliters (approx.)
1 fluid ounce = 29.6 milliliters
1 cup = .24 liter
1 pint = .47 liter
1 quart = .95 liter
1 pound = .45 kilogram

Conversion from Fahrenheit to Celsius:
subtract 32 and then multiply the remainder by 5/9

LIBRARY OF CONGRESS CATALOGING-IN-PUBLICATION DATA
Stamper, Judith Bauer.
   Thanksgiving holiday grab bag / by Judith Stamper; illustrated by
Ann Iosa.
     p.   cm.
   Summary: Discusses the origin of Thanksgiving and suggests various
activities for the holiday.
   ISBN 0-8167-2906-9 (lib. bdg.)   ISBN 0-8167-2907-7 (pbk.)
1. Thanksgiving decorations—Juvenile literature. 2. Thanksgiving
Day—Juvenile literature. 3. Thanksgiving cookery—Juvenile
literature. [1. Thanksgiving Day.] I. Iosa, Ann, ill. II. Title.
TT900.T5S73   1993
745.594'1—dc20   92-13420

Copyright © 1993 by Troll Associates.
All rights reserved. No part of this book may be used or reproduced in
any manner whatsoever without written permission from the publisher.
Printed in the United States of America.
10 9 8 7 6 5 4 3 2 1

Contents

Introduction   4

Facts About the Pilgrims   6

Pilgrims All   8

Pilgrim Wit   10

Thanksgiving Banner   11

Turkey Trivia   16

Turkey Treats   18

Facts About the Native Americans   20

Sign Language of the Native Americans   22

Moccasins   26

Corny Jokes   29

Seeds for Survival   30

Johnnycakes   32

Cornhusk Dolls   34

Thanksgiving Magic   36

Science in the Kitchen   38

Cranberries   40

Toothpick Tricks   42

Thanksgiving Trivia Quiz   45

A Funny Feast   47

Happy Thanksgiving   48

Introduction

🎩 Thanksgiving is a truly American holiday. Its traditions began in the New World with the feast shared by the Pilgrims and Native Americans. All its food is American, from Tom Turkey to Cape Cod cranberries. And its spirit is all American, too — football games, parades, and family fun!

How did this special holiday begin? In 1620, a ship called the *Mayflower* brought 102 English settlers to America. Some of these settlers were Pilgrims, who came to the New World to practice their religious beliefs in freedom. Others came for adventure or a new start in life.

    The Pilgrim settlers at Plymouth, Massachusetts, barely survived their first winter in the New World. But with the help of the Native Americans who lived in the area, they reaped a bountiful corn crop the next autumn.
    The Pilgrims decided to have a three-day celebration feast to give thanks for a good harvest. Thus began the first Thanksgiving. The settlers' Native American friends came to share the feast. Long tables set outside were piled with food. Everyone danced, sang, and ate.
    Throughout American history, people have found reasons to give thanks for peace and prosperity. Over the years, we have remembered the first Thanksgiving: the Pilgrims, the Native Americans, the *Mayflower*, and a delicious feast.
    The stories, crafts, recipes, and games in this book are about Thanksgiving past and present. They will help make this holiday a very special one for you.

Facts About the Pilgrims

🎩 The Pilgrims settled at Plymouth Plantation along Cape Cod Bay in what is now Massachusetts.

🎩 Two children were born aboard the *Mayflower*. They were Oceanus Hopkins and Peregrine (meaning "pilgrim") White.

🎩 During the first hard winter and spring at Plymouth, half the original settlers died.

🎩 The Pilgrims did not always dress in drab colors as is commonly believed. From records of their wills, describing articles of clothing to be given to their families, we can see that they wore colorful clothing. The women and girls wore dresses of blue, green, purple, and red. One man owned a violet cloak, a red cap, and a green pair of trousers. And there is no historical proof that the Pilgrims wore buckles on their shoes or hats!

🎩 Most Pilgrim children had common names like Mary or John. But several had names that showed their parents' values and beliefs, such as Resolved White, Humility Cooper, and Love Brewster.

🎩 During their three-day Thanksgiving feast, the Pilgrims ate and made merry. They were not so different from you and your family.

Pilgrims All

The word *pilgrim* means "one who journeys to a foreign land." The Pilgrims who came on the *Mayflower* were among the first European settlers in America. But millions of immigrants followed them to this country in later years.

Your ancestors who first came to the United States were pilgrims, too. How much do you know about them? Thanksgiving is a good time to learn more.

If you are having a family get-together, talk with your older relatives about the family's past. If you won't see your relatives in person, write them a letter with questions, or talk to them on the telephone. Families sometimes forget to write down their histories. If you don't do it now, important memories may be lost!

Questions To Ask

1. What were the names of our ancestors who first came to America?

2. In what years did they immigrate?

3. From what countries did they come?

4. What stories have you heard about them?

5. Do you have any pictures of them, or things that belonged to them?

    These questions are just the beginning. Once your mother, father, aunts, uncles, grandmothers, or grandfathers start talking, they'll tell you much more. It is important for you to record what they say. The easiest way to do this is with a tape recorder. Or you can carefully write down the important facts. Ask your parents to help you make a record of all the members of your family, going back as far as anyone can remember.

    Sharing your "pilgrim past" is a sure way to give your family a happy Thanksgiving.

Pilgrim Wit

If a man was born in England, came to America, and died at Plymouth Rock, what is he?

Dead

If April showers bring May flowers, what do Mayflowers bring?

Pilgrims

What kind of dance did the Pilgrims do?

The Plymouth Rock

What do you call Thanksgiving dinner in a hayloft?

Turkey in the Straw

Thanksgiving Banner

You can add to the holiday mood in your house with this easy project. Begin by making a colorful crayon drawing of the Thanksgiving pictures shown on these pages. Next, you'll transfer your drawing to fabric with a warm iron. The finished product can be a large place mat for the center of your Thanksgiving table or a pretty Thanksgiving banner.

Materials

Crayons
Typing paper
Pencil
Cloth
Iron and ironing board
Scissors

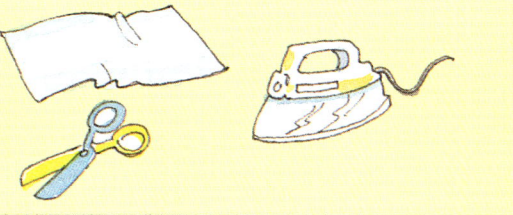

Steps

1. Choose one of the designs shown on these pages. Place a piece of typing paper over it, and trace the design with a pencil. Trace more designs if you want, and combine them in a pretty pattern.

continued...

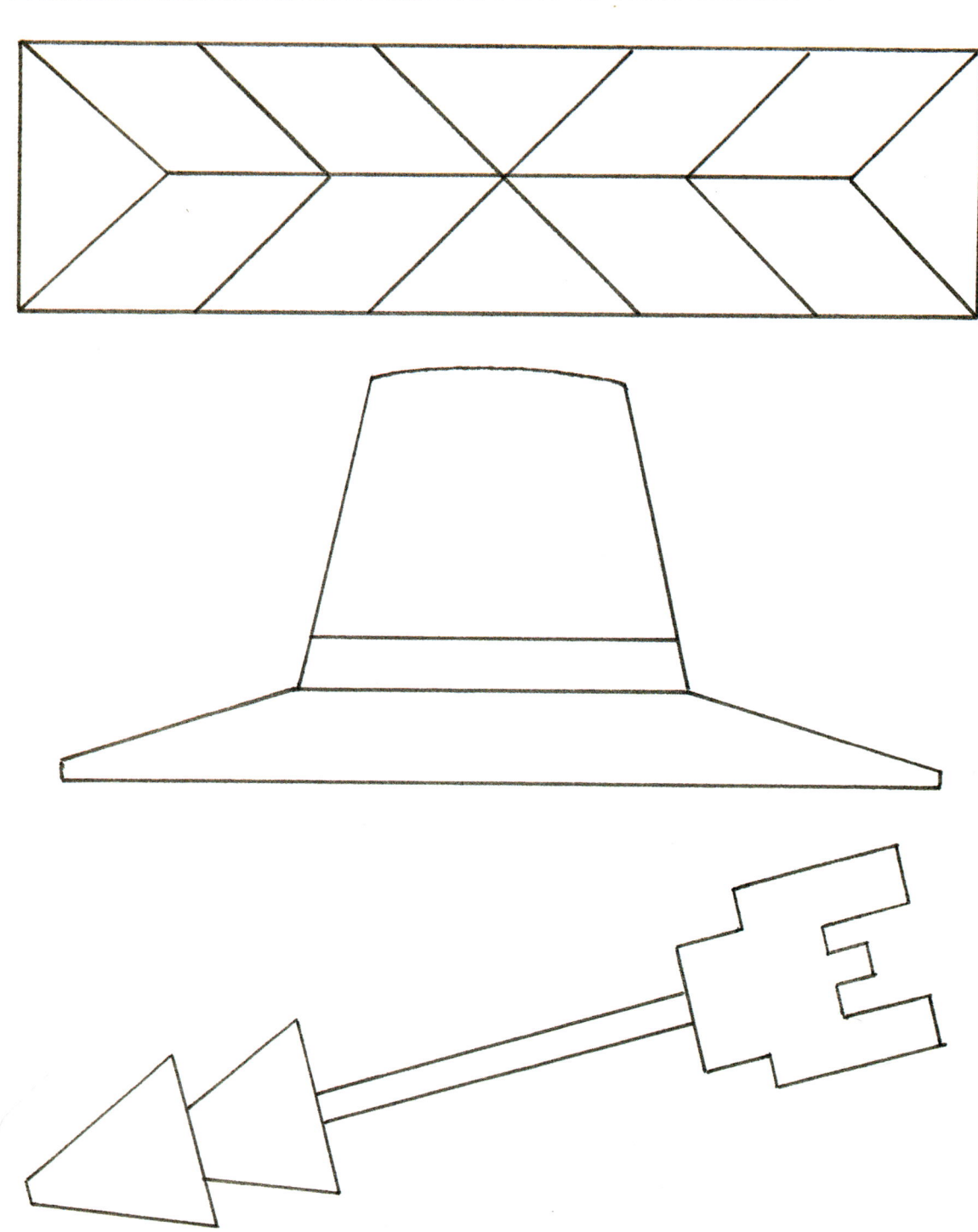

2. Color the design with bright crayons, pressing hard to get a deep, even color.

3. Cut a piece of plain cloth to the size you need. A white background works well to show off your design. If you want, you can fringe or hem the edges of the cloth.

13

continued...

4. With the help of an adult, heat an iron to the temperature suggested for the type of cloth you are using. Put your drawing, crayon side down, on the cloth. Iron over the paper, letting the crayon melt into the cloth. (*Note:* Keep moving the iron over the design so the paper does not become scorched.)

5. Pull the paper off the cloth. Your crayon design is finished!

These easy steps give you a beautiful fabric design that is permanent and can be washed. Your place mat or banner will add a special touch to Thanksgiving this year.

Turkey Trivia

Americans eat over 75 million turkeys each year, most of them at Thanksgiving time.

The Cheyenne people would not eat turkey. They believed it would make them cowards, like the turkey who runs away whenever threatened.

A male turkey is called a tom. A female turkey is called a hen. Young turkeys are called poults.

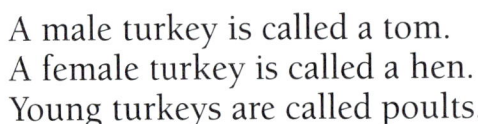

Turkey eggs are twice as big as chicken eggs.

The fold of skin at the front of a turkey's neck is called its wattle.

The turkey is native to North and South America — the only kind of poultry that is.

A wild turkey can fly up to 55 miles per hour.

The largest turkey can weigh up to 50 pounds.

 # Turkey Treats

These turkey treats are as much fun to eat as they are to make. You can serve them to friends as a snack. Or you can make them for your guests at Thanksgiving dinner. The turkeys can even hold place cards.

You Will Need

Medium-size red apples
Box of raisins
Jar of medium-size green stuffed olives
Toothpicks

Steps

1. Wash and polish an apple. Remove the stem. This will be the body of your turkey.

2. Fill a toothpick with raisins, leaving small space at each end. Stick one end of the toothpick into the top center of the apple.

3. Use a green olive for the turkey's head. Remove the red pimento from inside and unfold it. Put the pimento back inside again, but leave half dangling out, like a turkey's wattle. Attach the olive to the top of the toothpick you've just inserted.

18

4. Use four toothpicks to make the turkey's legs. Push two in at the same place on each side of the bottom of the apple, but bring the toothpicks out at angles so they support the turkey. Push a raisin onto the ends of each of the "feet."

5. Fill five more toothpicks with raisins, leaving a small space free at one end. Push them into the top back of the apple to look like a turkey's fanned tail feathers.

6. Break two toothpicks in half, and fill the four halves with raisins. Stick these shorter feathers into the sides of the apples.

Your turkey treat is finished. Your friends and guests will agree that it's a gobbler worth gobbling!

Facts About the Native Americans

🍂 The Native Americans who came to the Thanksgiving feast at Plymouth were members of the Wampanoag (wam-puh-NO-ag) nation. Chief Massasoit, their leader, arrived at the feast with 90 of his people. The Wampanoag smoked their pipes, tasted English cooking, and presented a dance to the Pilgrims.

🍂 Wampanoag men living near Plymouth wore deerskin aprons in warm weather. In cold weather, they wore deerskin leggings, moccasins, and mantles. They often wore an eagle feather in their hair.

🍂 Wampanoag women wore deerskin dresses and moccasins. Their long hair was worn braided. Jewelry was made of shells, and coats were made of deerskin or beaver fur.

History Mystery

What do you know about the Native American nations in your area of the United States? Your local library will have books explaining which nations have lived in the different regions of the country. The librarian may have more specific information about your area's local history. Be a history detective. Find out as much as you can about your region and its customs.

Sign Language of the Native Americans

Samoset was the first Native American to greet the Pilgrims. He walked into the Plymouth settlement, saying "Welcome, Englishmen." Samoset had learned the Pilgrims' language from English fishermen. But communication was not always so easy.

Just as each nation had its own customs, each had its own language. A common way of communicating grew among the Native Americans. This was sign language. It was soon learned by the settlers.

On the following pages are several examples of sign language. Try them out on your friends and family on Thanksgiving Day.

Man Place right hand in front of chest and point index finger up. Move hand up in front of face.

Boy Sign **Man**. Then use flat, right hand to show height.

Woman Curve in fingers of both hands. As if combing long hair, move hands from top of head to shoulders.

Girl Sign **Woman**. Then use flat, right hand to show height.

Father Close fingers of right hand. Touch right side of chest several times.

Mother Close fingers of right hand. Touch left side of chest several times.

continued...

Brother Raise index and second fingers and touch lips. Then move hand straight away from mouth. Then sign **Man**.

Sister Sign **Woman**. Raise index and second fingers and touch lips. Then move hand straight away from mouth.

I Point to self with right thumb.

You Point to person with right thumb.

Eat Cup right hand. Move up and down in front of mouth.

Full (Eat Enough) Sign **Eat**. Spread index finger and thumb of right hand apart. Move right hand from chest to chin.

Thank You Raise both hands to shoulders with palms facing out. Lower hands in a curve toward person to be thanked.

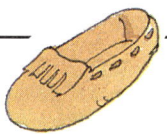 # Moccasins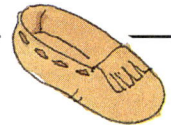

The Native Americans who came to the first Thanksgiving feast at Plymouth wore moccasins made of deerskin. Such shoes were perfect for travel in the American wilderness. Moccasins were lightweight and soft, making it easy to move quietly and surely over slippery ledges and rocks.

The instructions below teach you how to make a pair of moccasins much like the ones the Native Americans wore. This Thanksgiving, feel what it is like to wear shoes you made yourself!

Materials

Pencil
Paper
Scissors
Strong needle and heavy thread
Felt or suede-like material
Shoelaces or string
Beads or markers

Steps

1. Fold a sheet of paper in half and place either foot half an inch from folded edge. Draw the outline of your foot on the paper.

2. Draw another line half an inch from footprint, as shown. Cut the pattern out along this line.

3. Unfold the pattern and lay it out on your moccasin material. Carefully cut out two of the pattern.

4. Fold each moccasin in half, inside out. Stitch around the front edges of the moccasins with a needle and thread, as shown. Turn the moccasins right side out with stitching face up, down the center.

5. For each moccasin, cut along the dotted lines pictured here. Remember to make one of the moccasins for the left foot and one for the right.

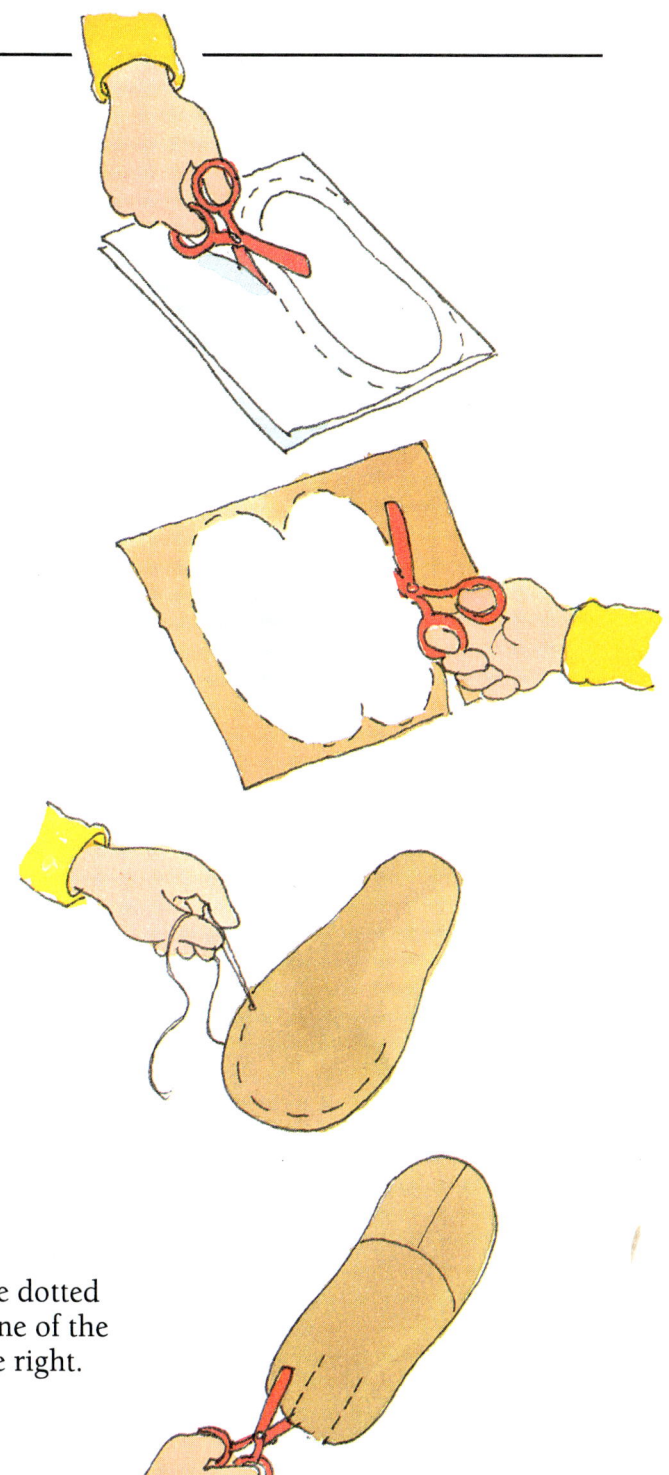

6. Put on the moccasins and wrap the 2 side flaps over the center flap as shown to fit them to your heels. Then sew the 3 flaps together.

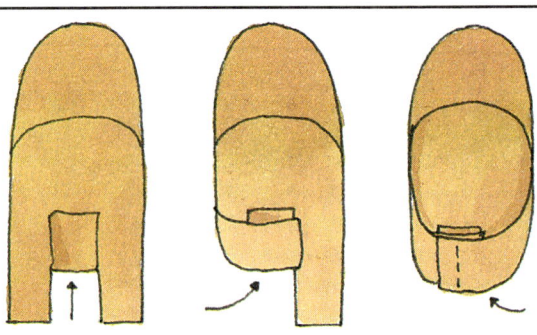

7. Cut a tongue from material to fit in front of each moccasin. Sew them in place.

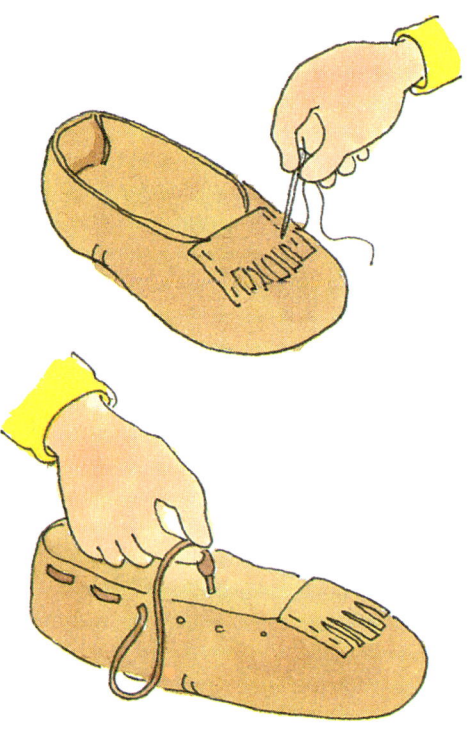

8. Make slits in the moccasins where shown, for laces to be threaded through. Laces can be made from material or from heavy string.

9. Decorate your moccasins with beads or markers, if you like. Or wear them plain and proud!

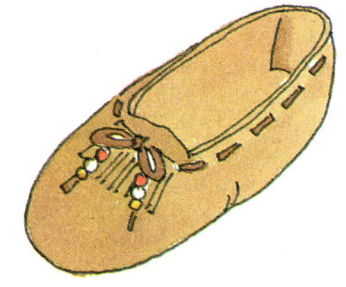

Corny Jokes

I have ears, but I can't hear. What am I?

A cornstalk

What did the little ear of corn call his father?

Pop Corn

Why did the cornstalk go to the doctor?

He had an earache.

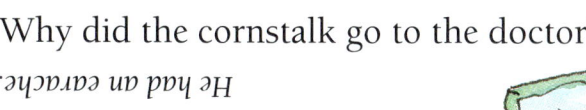

What do you get from an ear of corn with dandruff?

Corn flakes

Seeds for Survival

During their first hard year in America, the Pilgrims found corn buried in the sand of Cape Cod. The corn had been stored there by the Native Americans. This important find gave the Pilgrims seeds to plant — and these became the seeds for survival. Without the harvest of corn they reaped from these seeds, the Pilgrims all could have died.

We usually do not watch seeds grow because they are buried underground. But it is possible to watch the process by using a glass germinator jar, in which the seeds sprout. This experiment is fun to do at Thanksgiving time using kernels of popcorn.

Seed Germinator

Materials

Medium or large glass jar with a wide mouth
Paper towel
5 to 10 popcorn kernels
Scissors
Water

Steps

1. Soak the kernels in water for four hours or overnight.

2. Trim the paper towel so it will fit inside the jar, as shown. Moisten the towel slightly to keep it in place. Then slip it around the inside of the jar.

3. Add about an inch of water to the bottom of the jar to keep the paper towel moist.

4. Slip the kernels between the paper towel and the side of the jar.

5. Within a week, you can watch your kernels grow into corn plants.

Why It Happens

The wet paper towel provides the moisture the kernels need to grow. First, the kernel swells until its outside covering bursts open. Then it sends its roots downward. Its stem and leaves are sent up to the top of the jar. Where does the corn seed get the nutrients to do this? This first growth can all be done with the food stored inside the seed itself.

If you would like to grow your seedlings, transplant them into a pot filled with soil. If you take good care of them, you will have your very own corn to eat on Thanksgiving.

Johnnycakes

The settlers soon learned to use cornmeal to make their bread, just as the Native Americans did. In New England, the favorite recipe for cornbread came to be known as johnnycakes. These small cakes, which are really like cornmeal pancakes, are easy to make. With an adult's help in using the stove, you can whip up this Thanksgiving treat for your whole family.

You Will Need

1 cup yellow cornmeal
1/2 teaspoon salt
1 cup boiling water
1/2 cup milk
Butter or cooking oil

Mixing bowl
Spoon
Large frying pan
Spatula
Measuring cup and spoons

Steps

1. Combine the cornmeal and salt in a mixing bowl.

2. Ask an adult to help you add the boiling water to the mixture. Stir until smooth. Add the milk and stir well.

3. Coat a frying pan with butter or oil. Put on stove over medium-low heat.

4. Drop tablespoons of the cornmeal mixture into the pan. Let the johnnycakes cook until golden brown, about 5 minutes. Flip the cakes over with a spatula. Brown on the other side.

5. Serve the cakes warm. Add butter and maple syrup, if you like. The cakes can also be eaten later when cold.

 # Cornhusk Dolls

The next time you buy fresh ears of corn, save the husks. You can use them to make cornhusk dolls like the ones Native American and Pilgrim children played with. These dolls are plain and simple, but they are special because you made them yourself. If you like, you can use the dolls as part of your family's Thanksgiving decorations.

Materials

Cornhusks
Lightweight string
Tempera paint and brush (or markers)
Fabric
Yarn
Glue
Scissors

Steps

1. If the husks are dried out, soak them in water until they are soft enough to bend.

2. Lay three cornhusks on top of each other and cut off the ends to make them even. Fold the husks in half. Then tie a string about one inch down from the fold to make a head.

34

3. To make arms, place two cornhusks on top of each other. Cut the ends so the husks are about four inches long. Tie strings a short distance from both ends to make hands. Slip the arms through the middle of the doll just below the head.

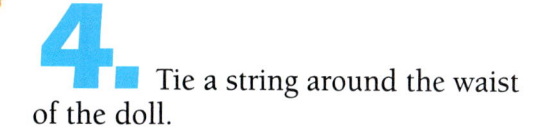

4. Tie a string around the waist of the doll.

5. To make a boy doll, cut the husks up to about an inch from the waist. Pull the husks apart to make two legs. Tie strings around the bottoms to make feet.

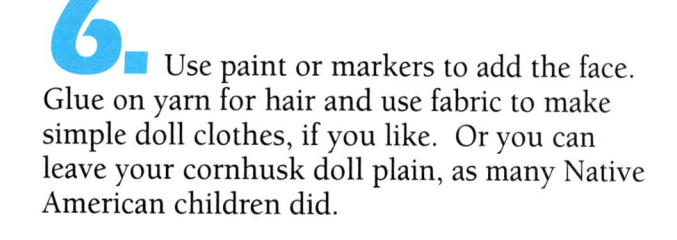

6. Use paint or markers to add the face. Glue on yarn for hair and use fabric to make simple doll clothes, if you like. Or you can leave your cornhusk doll plain, as many Native American children did.

35

Thanksgiving Magic

Add some magic to your Thanksgiving with these amazing tricks. All you need is a calendar, a pencil, and note paper.

The Magic

Open a calendar to November and give it, along with a pencil, to a friend. Ask the person to secretly circle any three dates that fall one after the other. The dates must be in one of the rows going across the calendar.

Now ask the person to add the three dates together and tell you the sum. A minute later, you will announce the three secret dates!

The Math

Divide the sum by 3. The answer will be the middle date. Subtract 1 from this date to get the first date. Add 1 to the middle date to get the last date.

More Magic

Hand the calendar and pencil to another person. Tell your friend to choose any month. Then ask the person to secretly circle three dates next to each other in one of the rows going down the calendar.

Now ask the person to add the three dates together and tell you the sum. A minute later, you will announce the three secret dates!

The Math

Divide the sum by 3. The answer will be the middle date. Subtract 7 from this number to get the first date. Add 7 to the middle date to get the last date.

Science in the Kitchen

Thanksgiving time can give you a chance to do a fun science experiment. It shows how plants send water from their roots to their leaves. All you need is some celery and food coloring. Be ready to show your interesting and colorful results to your guests on Thanksgiving Day.

Striped Celery

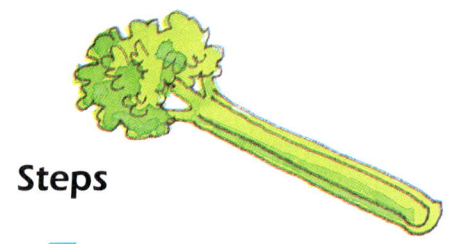

You Will Need

Stalk of celery, 9–10 inches high
Two water glasses, 4–5 inches high
Two colors of food coloring
Knife

Steps

1. Cut off half an inch from the root end of the celery stalk. Then, beginning from the root end, slice the stalk down the middle going about half way up. (*Note:* Ask an adult for help if you're not allowed to use a knife by yourself.)

2. Fill each glass with water. Add a different color of food coloring to each glass. For example, add red to one and blue to the other. Set the glasses side by side.

3. Put half of the celery stalk in each of the glasses. Let stand for about two hours.

4. After two hours, your celery stalk will have streaks of blue coming up one side and streaks of red coming up the other. Remove the celery from the water and cut across the stalk. You will see dots of color at the end you have cut.

Why It Happens

The celery has a system of tubes running up from its roots to its leaves. When the celery is growing, these tubes supply the plant with water drawn from the ground. The food coloring dyed the tubes, letting you see how the plant carried its water supply.

Cranberries

The Native Americans living around Cape Cod called them *ibimi*, meaning "bitter berries." The Pilgrims named them *crane berries,* because their blossoms look like the heads of cranes. In time, the name was shortened to *cranberry*. Today, no Thanksgiving table is complete without these festive berries.

The Native Americans found many uses for the wild berries. The juice made a red dye for rugs and blankets. The mashed berries helped draw poison out of arrow wounds. Ibimi mixed with venison made a preserved food that would last a long time.

Pilgrim women also invented many ways to sweeten the bitter berries for food. The most popular recipe passed down from them is cranberry sauce. This dish is simple to make and can be your contribution to the family Thanksgiving feast.

Cranberry Sauce with Orange

You Will Need

1 pound fresh cranberries
1-1/2 cups sugar
2 cups water
1 large orange
Saucepan
Colander
Spoon
Measuring cup
Knife
Potholder

Steps

1. Wash the cranberries well. Throw away any that are soft or discolored.

2. Peel the orange and remove the seeds. Chop the orange into small pieces. (*Note*: Ask an adult for help, if you're not allowed to use a knife by yourself.)

3. Combine the sugar and water in a saucepan. With the help of an adult, bring it to a boil.

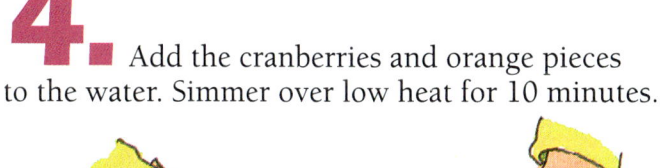

4. Add the cranberries and orange pieces to the water. Simmer over low heat for 10 minutes.

5. Skim off the white foam from the top of the sauce. Remember to use a potholder when handling the pan. Let the mixture cool.

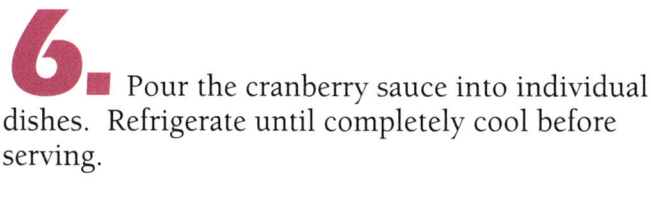

6. Pour the cranberry sauce into individual dishes. Refrigerate until completely cool before serving.

Toothpick Tricks

After a big Thanksgiving dinner, most people are too full to move. You can help entertain everyone with these brain teasers. They require only one prop — a box of toothpicks.

Here are four toothpick tricks. Try to figure them out yourself before turning the page to see the answers.

A. Arrange 12 toothpicks, as shown.

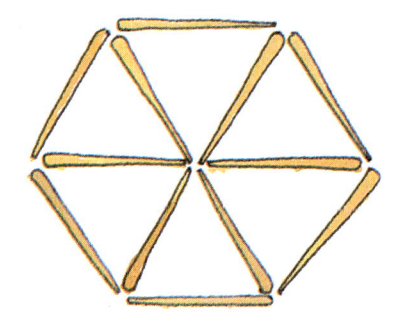

The challenge: Moving only 4 of the toothpicks already on the table, create 3 triangles out of this shape.

B. Arrange 7 toothpicks into a triangle, as shown.

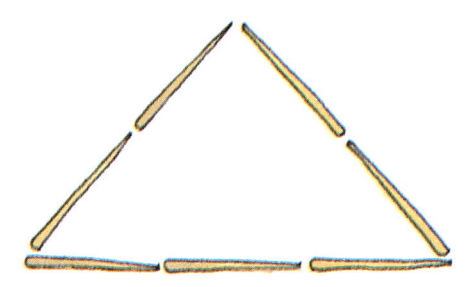

The challenge: Moving only 3 of the toothpicks, create 3 connected triangles.

42

C. Arrange 15 toothpicks, as shown.

The challenge: Remove 6 toothpicks from the design and still leave 10.

D. Arrange 12 toothpicks in 4 connected squares, as shown.

The challenge: Moving only 3 toothpicks, create 3 squares.

continued...

Answers

A.

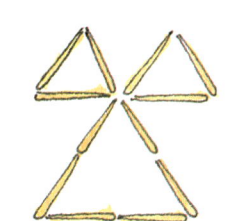

B.

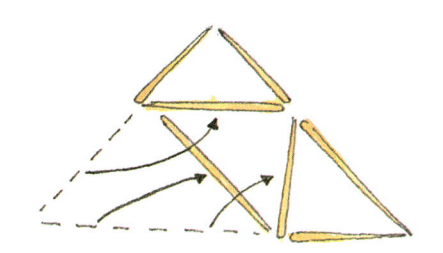

C.

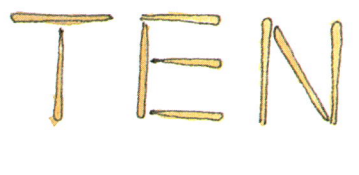

D.

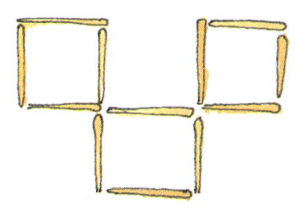

44

Thanksgiving Trivia Quiz

1. What day does Thanksgiving fall on each year?
2. What is the most popular Thanksgiving dessert?
3. Where does the big Thanksgiving parade in New York City end?
4. In what song does the line: "Land of the Pilgrims' pride" appear?
5. What is a cornucopia?
6. What is the name of the place where the Pilgrims stepped ashore from the *Mayflower*?
7. Who is the Native American who lived with the Pilgrims and taught them his ways?
8. What was the Native American name for corn?

(If you're stuck, turn the page to find the answers.)

Answers

1. Thanksgiving takes place on the fourth Thursday in November.

2. Pumpkin pie is the most popular.

3. The parade ends at Macy's department store, the sponsor of the parade.

4. The song is "America" ("My country 'tis of thee . . .").

5. A cornucopia is a horn of plenty, filled with the fruits and vegetables of the harvest season.

6. They stepped ashore at Plymouth Rock.

7. The Native American was Squanto.

8. The Native Americans called corn *maize*.

A Funny Feast

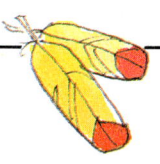

Why shouldn't you feed a Thanksgiving turkey?

Because it's already stuffed.

Why were screams coming from the kitchen on Thanksgiving Day?

The cook was beating the eggs and whipping the potatoes.

Where does Superman go to buy his Thanksgiving feast?

To a supermarket.

Which weighs more: a pound of turkey or a pound of cranberries?

They both weigh a pound.

Happy Thanksgiving!